RISQUÉ JOKES

ISBN: 1 84161 217 0

This edition first published by Ravette Publishing in 2004.

Printed and bound in Malaysia
for Ravette Publishing Limited
Unit 3, Tristar Centre, Star Road, Partridge Green,
West Sussex RH13 8RA
United Kingdom

RISQUÉ JOKES

RR
RAVETTE PUBLISHING

Introduction

There is nothing better than a good dose of humour to brighten any day. Okay, well, we know food and shelter and health and love and world peace all have their places, but they don't exactly make you laugh in any sidesplitting way. They don't tickle your funny bone like a good joke might. In fact, it would be a pretty strange world without laughter, and everyone would go about with long, serious faces, wondering when someone was going to invent humour. There'd be no, "Why did the chicken cross the road?" or "Did you hear the one about …" The only laughter would be coming from hyenas and God knows what they would find funny.

We titled this collection Risqué Jokes because we thought you would be embarrassed to be seen reading a book titled Rude Jokes. But don't worry, only the title has changed, the jokes are just as you like them. You should be ashamed! To save you feeling really sleazy we have included a number of clean jokes so you can always say you bought the book for those.

Things a man shouldn't say to a woman during sex:

Oops! It seems to have come off.
If you come quick, I can catch the game on TV.
You look just like your mother.
You're better than your mother.
Did you remember to lock the back door?
And to think, I was really trying to pick up your friend!
You carry on, but do you mind if I finish this book?
What's for dinner tomorrow?
I thought you had the keys to the handcuffs.
It's my mobile! I must answer it.
I can see right up your nose.
Oh, by the way, the cat got run over this afternoon.
That boil on your chin looks nasty.
Did I tell you my aunt Agatha died in this bed?
Linda used to do that.
Do you accept Visa?
It's nice being in bed with a woman I don't have to inflate.
"I keep having fantasies about Barbara Bush,"
"Did I mention the video camera?"

"Hurry up—this room rents by the hour. "
"Sorry about that—must be the baked beans."
"This would be fun with a few more people."
"Try not to leave any stains, OK?"
"I've just thought of the answer to 3 down. I won't be a second."
"Shall I do my impression of Officer Dibble?"
"Do you know the definition of statutory rape?"
"Keep it down. My mother is a light sleeper,"
"I see that mad axeman's still on the loose."
"Is that it? Can I go now?"

* * * * *

Things a woman shouldn't say to a man during sex:

"And yet your feet are so big!"
"Don't worry, we'll work around it."
"I guess this makes me the early bird."
"Try not to smear my make-up."
"At least this won't take long."
"I want a baby."
"Do you know the ceiling needs painting?"

"Maybe we should call Dr Ruth."
"Is that blood on the headboard?"
"Did I remember to take my pill?"
"It's just a rash."
"Sorry about the name tags, but I'm not very good with names."
"Does it come with an air pump?"
"But it still works, right?"
"Why don't we skip right to the cigarettes?"
"But everybody looks funny naked."
"Do you smell something burning?"
"On second thoughts, let's turn off the lights."
"You must be cold."
"Don't mind me. I always file my nails in bed,"
"Maybe if we water it, it'll grow."
"Maybe it looks better in natural light,"
"Maybe you're just out of practice."
"When is this supposed to feel good?"
"It's a good thing you're rich."

Why did God create women?
To carry semen from the bedroom to the toilet.

If the dove is the bird of peace, what is the bird of true love?
The swallow.

How do you annoy your girlfriend during sex?
Phone her.

Why do women fake orgasms?
Because they think men care.

What's the definition of 'making love'?
Something a woman does while a guy is f***ing her.

What should you do if your girlfriend starts smoking?
Slow down and use a lubricant.

Whats the difference between oral sex and anal sex?
Oral sex makes your day, anal sex makes your hole weak.

Why does a bride always wear white?
Because it's good for the dishwasher to match the stove and the fridge.

What do you say to a woman with two black eyes?
Nothing, she's been told twice already.

How do you turn a fox into an elephant?
Marry it.

What is the difference between a battery and a woman?
A battery has a positive side.

What are the three fastest means of communication?
Internet, telephone, telawoman.

Why do hunters make the best lovers?
Because they go deep in the bush, shoot more than once and they eat what they shoot.

How are fat girls and mopeds alike?
They're both fun to ride until your friends find out.

How is a woman like a condom?
Both of them spend more time in your wallet than on your dick.

What should you give a woman who has everything?
A man to show her how to work it.

How are twisters (tornadoes) and marriage alike?
They both begin with a lot of blowing and sucking, and in the end you lose your house.

Why does a bride smile when she walks up the aisle?
She knows she's given her last blow job.

Whats the difference between your wife and your job?
After 10 years, the job still sucks.

Whats the definition of love, true love, and showing off?
Spitting, swallowing and gargling.

Why is the space between a woman's breasts and her hips called a waist?
Because you could easily fit another pair of tits in there.

Do you know why they call it the Wonder Bra?
When you take it off you wonder where her tits went.

A fireman and his wife were bored with their sex life so he tried to liven it up by incorporating the bell system that was used at work. At the firehouse when the first bell rings, everyone runs to the trucks; on the second bell, they gear up; and on the third bell they jump on the trucks and head for the fire. So he went home and told his wife:

"I've got this great idea to spice up our sex life. We're gonna use the bell system. When I shout 'bell one', you run into the bedroom; when I shout 'bell two', you take off your clothes; and when I call 'bell three', you jump on the bed and we make passionate love."

The next evening he got home from work and immediately shouted 'bell one'. His wife ran into the bedroom. Then he called out 'bell two' and she took off her clothes. Then he yelled 'bell three' and the pair leaped on the bed together and started making love. But no sooner had they started than she suddenly cried: "Bell four, bell four!'

"What the hell's bell four?" he gasped.

"More hose! More hose! You're nowhere near the fire!"

A couple went to an agricultural show one weekend and watched the auction of some prize bulls. The auctioneer announced that the first bull had reproduced 72 times last year. "Hey," said the wife, nudging her husband. "That's six times a month. A pity you can't match that." The next bull for auction was revealed to have reproduced 144 times last year. The wife prodded her husband again. "Did you hear that? Twelve times a month! He's way out of your league."

Then a third bull was led around. The auctioneer proudly stated that the animal had reproduced 365 times last year. The wife elbowed her husband hard in the ribs. "Three hundred and sixty-five times!" she exclaimed. "That's every day of the year. That really puts you to shame." By now, the husband was thoroughly irritated by the jibes. "Sure. Great," he said; icily. "But I bet it wasn't all with the same cow."

* * * * *

On the night before his wedding, the shy young man thought he ought to ask his father what was expected of him in the bedroom.

"What exactly do I have to do?" he asked tentatively.

"Well, Son," said his father. "You remember what you used to play with as a teenager? All you do is stick that where your wife pees." So the following night the young man threw G.I. Joe down the toilet.

* * * * *

A young couple on their first date had sex which was over in a matter of seconds. Feeling rather proud of himself, the boy said: "If I'd known you were a virgin, I'd have taken more time."

" The girl replied: "If I'd known you were going to take more time, I'd have taken off my panty hose."

* * * * *

A man living on the second storey of an apartment block was leaning out of the window one morning to check whether it was raining, when a glass eye suddenly fell into his hand. Looking up, he saw a girl peering down from four storey's above. "Is this yours?" he called out.

"Yes," she replied.

"Hold on," he said. "I'll bring it up to you." So he took the glass eye up to the girl's apartment. She invited him in and they started chatting. Not only was she extremely grateful to him but she also found him incredibly attractive and so she asked him out to dinner that evening. He readily accepted. The meal was a great success and afterwards she suggested they go back to his place and go to bed. She stayed the night and when she left the following morning, he said: "I'm sorry but I have to ask. Do you act like this with every man you meet?"

"No," she replied, "Only those who catch my eye."

* * * * *

The headmistress of a girls' school asked a male friend who was an author to give a talk to the pupils about sex. After much persuasion, the man agreed but was too embarrassed to tell his wife. So he told her that he was addressing the school on sailing and wrote an appropriate entry in his diary for that day. The day after the talk, the headmistress met the wife in the street. "Your husband was wonderful yesterday, so illuminating. I know my girls learned a lot from him."

"I can't think how," said the wife. "He's only tried it twice. The first time he was sick and the second time he lost his hat."

* * * * *

Q. How can you tell if a novel is homosexual?
A. The hero always gets his man in the end.

Q. How can you tell if a Western is homosexual?
A. All the good guys are hung.

Superman was bored because Batman and Spiderman were on vacation and there was nothing much to do. Flying around New York one day, he spotted Wonder Woman lying on her back with her legs apart on the roof of a tall building. He had always lusted after Wonder Woman so he thought he would swoop down and have his wicked way with her.
"What was that?" said Wonder Woman afterwards.
The Invisible Man climbed off her and said: "I dunno, but it hurt."

* * * * *

A male market researcher was calling on homes on behalf of Vaseline. A woman answered the door. "Do you use Vaseline?" asked the researcher.
"Certainly," she said. "It's very good for cuts, grazes and burns."
"And what about anything else?" he asked.
"Like what?" He became embarrassed. "Well, sex, maybe."
Oh, of course." she said. "I smear it on the bedroom doorknob to keep my husband out."

A guy and his date were parked on a back road way out of town. Things started to heat up and he began to undo her dress. "I probably should have mentioned this before," she said, "but I'm a prostitute and if you want to have sex with me, it will cost you twenty dollars."

The guy wasn't happy, but he paid up. Afterwards, he got dressed but just sat in the driver's seat without starting the engine.

"Why aren't we going anywhere?" asked the woman.

"I probably should have mentioned this before," he replied, "but I'm a taxi driver and if you want to get back to town, it will cost you thirty dollars!"

* * * * *

There was a young man named McSweeny
Who spilled some gin on his weenie
Just to be couth
He added Vermouth
And gave his girlfriend a martini!

A middle-aged man was told at the hospital that he had only 24 hours to live. He went home in a state of shock and fell into his wife's arms. "I've been told I've only got 24 hours to live," he said. "Can we have sex one last time?"

"Of course, honey," she said, and they went to bed.

Four hours later, he turned to her and said: "Could we have sex again? I've only got 20 hours to live. It will probably be our last chance."

"Sure, honey," replied his wife and they had sex.

Eight hours later, he asked her. "Do you think we could have sex one more time? After all, I've only got 12 hours to live."

"OK," said the wife and they had sex.

Four hours later, he nudged her in bed. "I just realised I've only got eight hours to live. Could we have sex one last time?"

"Very well," she sighed. "It's the least I can do in the circumstances".

Four hours later, he woke her again. "I've only got fours to live. Would you mind if we had sex just one more time, our final act of love?"

" This was too much for the wife. "Listen," she snapped, "you may not have to get up in the morning, but I do!"

* * * * *

A couple decided that the only way to have a quickie while their ten-year-old son was in the apartment was to send him out on the balcony and let him give a running report on what was going on in the neighbourhood. So the boy stood on the balcony and reported on everything that was happening. "A police car has just called at the Hamiltons' house, the Chandlers are taking delivery of a new wardrobe, and the Mitchell's are having sex." Hearing this, the boy's parents shot bolt upright. "How do you know the Mitchells are having sex?"

"Because their kid is standing on the balcony too."

With his wife away on an overseas trip, a guy decided to take his secretary back to his house for an evening of passion. They were rolling around on the bed when he suddenly remembered he didn't have any condoms. "What are we gonna do?" he said.

"I don't know," answered the secretary. "I don't have any either."

Just then he hit upon an idea. "Hey'" he yelled exultantly. "No problem. I know where my wife keeps her diaphragm. You can use that."

So he searched the top drawer of the dressing table where the wife always kept her contraceptive device but it was nowhere to be found. After 20 minutes, he gave up. "Goddam bitch!" he snarled. "She's taken it with her. I always knew she didn't trust me!"

* * * * *

A guy was told he had just 24 hours to live, so he decided to go home and make passionate love to his wife. He crept into the dark bedroom, slid into bed and for the next three hours enjoyed the wildest sex he'd ever experienced. Finally exhausted, he crawled into the bathroom where he was surprised to find his wife lying in the bath with a mudpack on her face.

"How did you get in here?" he asked.

"Sssh!" she said. "You'll wake my mother."

* * * * *

A woman went to the doctor and complained that she was suffering from knee pains.

"Do you indulge in any activity that puts a lot of pressure on your knees?" asked the doctor.

"Every night, my husband and I have sex on the floor doggy style."

"I see," said the doctor. "You know, there are plenty of other sexual positions?"

"Not if you want to watch TV there ain't!"

A truck driver was going down a steep incline when, at the foot of the hill, he was able to make out a couple having sex in the middle of the road. Five times on his descent he sounded his horn, but they didn't move. He finally brought the truck to a halt inches from them. The truck driver got out and stormed: "What the hell's the matter with you two? Didn't you hear me? You could have been killed!" The man replied nonchalantly: "Listen, I was coming, she was coming, and you were coming. You were the only one with brakes."

* * * * *

Pinocchio had been getting complaints from his girlfriend. "Every time we make love," she said, "I get splinters." So Pinocchio went back to his maker, Gipetto the carpenter, for advice.
"Sandpaper," said the carpenter. "That's what you need." So Pinocchio took some sheets of sandpaper and went home. A few weeks later the carpenter bumped into Pinocchio again.
"How are you getting on with the girls now?" he asked.
"Who needs girls?" said Pinocchio.

Q: How do you find a blind man in a nudist colony?
A: It's not hard.

Q: What's the difference between a girlfriend and a wife?
A: 45 lbs.

Q: What's the difference between a boyfriend and a husband?
A: 45 minutes.

Q: What is it when a man talks dirty to a woman?
A: Sexual harassment.

Q: What is it when a woman talks dirty to a man?
A: $3.99 a minute.

Q: How are women and rocks alike?
A: You skip across the flat ones.

Q: Did you hear about the new blonde paint?
A: It's not real bright, but it's cheap, and spreads easy.

Q: Whats the difference between a 90s woman and a computer?
A: A 90s woman won't accept a three-and-a-half-inch floppy.

Q: Why do men find it difficult to make eye contact?
A: Because breasts don't have eyes.

Q: What's the difference between a blonde and a brick?
A: When you lay a brick, it doesn't follow you around for two weeks whining.

Q: What's a blondes favourite nursery rhyme?
A: Hump-me Dump-me. "

Q: What's the difference between erotic and kinky?
A: Erotic is when you use a feather. Kinky is when you use the whole chicken.

Q: Why do Greek men wear gold neck chains?
A: So they know where to stop shaving.

Q: What is the difference between medium and rare?
A: Six inches is medium, eight inches is rare.

Q: Why don't men fake orgasm?
A: Coz no man would pull those faces on purpose.

Q: What are the small bumps around a woman s nipples for?
A: It's Braille for 'Suck here.'

Q: Why do most women pay more attention to their appearance than to improving their minds?
A: Because most men are stupid but few are blind.

Q: What does a 75-year-old woman have between her breasts that a 25-year-old doesn't?
A: Her navel.

Q: Why do women have tits?
A: So men will talk to them.

Q: Why do women rub their eyes when they get up in the morning?
A: They don't have balls to scratch.

Q: What's the difference between a pub and a clitoris?
A: A guy can find a pub.

Q: Whats the difference between purple and pink?
A: The grip.

* * * * *

Paddy and his two friends are talking at work. His first friend says, "I think my wife is having an affair with the electrician. The other day I came home and found wire cutters under our bed and they weren't mine."

His second friend says, "I think my wife is having an affair with the plumber. The other day I found a wrench under the bed and it wasn't mine."

Paddy says, "I think my wife is having an affair with a horse." Both his friends look at him with utter disbelief. "I'm serious. The other day I came home and found a jockey under our bed."

* * * * *

Two couples were playing cards. John accidentally dropped some cards on the floor. When he bent down under the table to pick them up, he noticed that Bill's wife wasn't wearing any underwear! Shocked by this, John hit his head on the table and emerged red-faced. Later, John went to the kitchen to get some refreshments. Bill's wife followed him and asked, "Did you see anything that you liked under there?"

John admitted that, well, yes, he did.

She said, "You can have it, but it will cost you $100." After a minute or two, John indicates that he is interested. She tells him that since Bill works Friday afternoons and John doesn't, John should come to her house around 2:00 pm on Friday. Friday came and John went to her house at 2:00 pm. After paying her $100 they went to the bedroom, had sex and then John left.

Bill came home about 6:00 pm. He asked his wife, "Did John come by this afternoon?"

Reluctantly, she replied, "Yes, he did stop by for a few minutes."

Next Bill asked, "Did John give you $100?"

She thinks, "Oh hell, he knows!" Finally she says, "Well, yes... he did give me $100."

"Good," Bill says. "John came by the office this morning and borrowed $100 from me. He said that he would stop by our house on his way home and pay me back."

* * * * *

A missionary suddenly realised that the one thing he hadn't yet taught the natives he served was how to speak English, so he takes the chief for a walk in the jungle. He points to a tree and says to the chief, "This is a tree." The chief looks at the tree and grunts, "Tree." The missionary is pleased with the response. They walk a little farther and the missionary points to a rock and says, "This is a rock." Hearing this, the chief looks and grunts, "Rock."

The missionary is really getting enthusiastic about the results when he hears a rustling in the bushes. As he peeks over the top, he sees a couple of the natives in the midst of heavy sexual activity. Flustered, the missionary quickly says to the chief, "Riding a bike." The chief looks at the preoccupied couple briefly, pulls out his blowgun and kills them. The missionary goes ballistic and yells at the chief that he has spent years teaching the tribe how to be civilised and kind to each other. "How could you kill these people in cold blood that way?" he demands.

"My bike," the chief replied.

Three women are discussing their teenage daughters. The first declares: "I was so shocked last week. I was tidying my daughter's room and I found a packet of cigarettes under her pillow. I didn't even know that she smoked!"

"It gets worse than that," says the second mother. "I was tidying my daughter's room last week and I found a bottle of vodka under her bed. I didn't even know that she drank!"

"Oh, it gets even worse than that," says the third mother. "I was tidying my daughter's room last week and you'll never guess what I found in her bedside cabinet: a packet of condoms!" I didn't even know that she had a penis!

* * * * *

There was a young lady from wheeling
Bereft of all sexual feeling
But when a young man named Boris
Patiently licked her clitoris
She had to be scraped off the ceiling.

If men got pregnant:

* Morning sickness would rank as the nation's number one health problem
* Maternity leave would last for two years with full pay
* Children would be kept in hospital until toilet trained
* Natural childbirth would become obsolete
* All methods of birth control would be 100 per cent effective
* Men would be eager to talk about commitment
* There would be a cure for stretch marks
* They'd serve beer instead of coffee at antenatal classes
* Men wouldn't think twins were so cute
* Sons would have to be home from dates by 10 p.m.

* * * * *

Jack and Tom, are having a beer in a saloon when a cowboy walks in with an Indian's head under his arm. He hands it to the bartender, and the bartender hands him money. The bartender turns to them and says, "I hate Indians. Last week they burnt my barn to the ground and killed my wife and three kids. Anybody brings me the head of an Indian, I'll give them a thousand bucks. "Jack and Tom guzzle their beers and leave to go hunt Indians. After a while, they finally spot one. Jack throws a rock, it hits him on the head, the Indian falls off his horse, and rolls seventy feet down a ravine. The two cowboys make their way down the ravine and Tom pulls out his knife to claim their trophy. Jack says, "Tom, take a look at this."

Tom says, "Not now, I'm busy."

Jack says, "I really think you should have a look."

Tom says, "Asshole, can't you see I'm busy? I've got a thousand dollars in my hand." Jack says,

"Please, Tom, take a look." Tom looks up at the top of the ravine, and there's five thousand Indians standing there. Tom says, "Fuck! We're gonna be millionaires!"

Two casino dealers are at the craps table when a cute blonde comes over and says, "I want to bet twenty thousand dollars on a single roll of the dice. But, if you don't mind, I'd feel much luckier if I were completely nude." They say fine, she strips naked from the neck down, and rolls the dice. Then she screams, "I won! I won!" She starts jumping up and down, hugs each of the dealers, and then picks up her money and her clothes and walks away. For a minute the two dealers stare at each other. Then the first one says, "What did she roll, anyway?"

The second dealer says, "I don't know. I thought you were watching."

* * * * *

A guy's talking to a girl in a bar.
He says, "What's your name?"
She says, "Carmen."
He says, "That's a nice name. Who named you, your mother?"
She says, "No, I named myself."

He says, "Why Carmen?"
She says, "Because I like cars and I like men. What's your name?"
He says, "Beerfuck."

* * * * *

Two snakes were slithering through a field. One snake turned to the other and asked, "Do you suppose we are poisonous?"
"I don't know", replied the other, "Why?"
"Well," said the first, "I just bit my lip!"

A teacher gave her fifth grade class an assignment: Get their parents to tell them a story with a moral at the end of it. The next day the kids came back and one by one began to tell their stories. Kathy said, "My father's a farmer and we have a lot of egg-laying hens. One time we were taking our eggs to market in a basket on the front seat of the pickup when we hit a bump in the road and all the eggs went flying and broke and made a mess."
"And what's the moral of the story?" asked the teacher.
"Don't put all your eggs in one basket!"
"Very good," said the teacher.

Next little Lucy raised a hand and said, "Our family are farmers, too. But we raise chickens for the meat market. We had a dozen eggs one time, but when they hatched we only got ten live chicks and the moral to this story is, don't count your chickens until they're hatched."
"That was a fine story Lucy. Johnny, do you have a story to share?"

"Yes, ma'am! My daddy told me this story about my Aunt Marge. She was a flight engineer during Desert Storm and her plane got hit. She had to bail out over enemy territory, and all she had was a bottle of whiskey, a machine gun and a Machete. So, she drank the whiskey on the way down so it wouldn't break. Then she landed right in the middle of 100 enemy troops. She killed 70 of them with the machine gun until it ran out of bullets! Then she killed 20 more with the machete till the blade broke; then she killed the last 10 with her bare hands."

"Good heavens," said the horrified teacher, "what kind of moral did your daddy tell you from that horrible story?"

"Stay away from Aunt Marge when she's been drinking."

* * * * *

My god! What happened to you?" the bartender asked Kelly as he hobbled in on a crutch, one arm in a cast.

"I got in a tiff with Riley."

"Riley? He's just a wee fellow," the barkeep said surprised.

"He must have had something in his hand."

"That he did," Kelly said. "A shovel it was."

"Dear Lord. Didn't you have anything in your hand?"

"Aye, that I did—Mrs. Riley's left tit." Kelly said. "And a beautiful thing it was, but not much use in a fight!"

Q. What doesn't belong in this list : Meat, Eggs, Wife, Blowjob?

A. Blowjob: You can beat your meat, eggs or wife, but you can't beat a blowjob.

Q. What do you call kids born in whorehouses?

A. Brothel sprouts.

Q. How do you know when you are getting old?

A. When you start having dry dreams and wet farts.

Q. What's the definition of a Yankee?

A. Same thing as a 'quickie', only you do it yourself.

Q. Why don't little girls fart?

A. Because they don't get assholes until they're married.

Q. Why do women stop bleeding when entering the menopause?

A. Because they need all the blood for their varicose veins !

* * * * *

There were two old-maid sisters... both virgins. It's Friday night and Gladys looks at Betty and says, "I'm not going to die a virgin... I'm going out and I'm not coming home 'til I've been laid!!"

Betty says, "Well, make sure you're home by 10.00 so I don't worry about you."

10 o'clock rolls around and there's no sign of Gladys... 11 o'clock...12 o'clock...

Finally about 1.00 the front door flys open. In runs Gladys... straight to the bathroom.

Betty goes and knocks on the door, "Are you okay, Gladys?"

No answer, so she opens the door and there sits Gladys with her panties around her ankles, legs spread, and her head stuck between her legs looking at herself.

"What is it, Gladys? What's wrong?" asks Betty.

"Betty, it was 10 inches long when it went in... and 5 when it came out. When I find the other half you're gonna have the time of your life!!!"

There is an 80 year old virgin who suddenly gets an itch in her crotch area. She goes to the doctor who checks her out and tells her she has crabs. She explained that she couldn't have crabs because she was a virgin, but the doctor didn't believe her, so she went to get a second opinion.

The second doctor gave her the same answer. So she went to a third doctor and said "Please help me. This itch is killing me and I know that I don't have crabs because I'm a virgin".

The doctor checks her out and says "I have good news and bad news. The good news is you don't have crabs, the bad news is that your cherry rotted and you have fruit flies."

* * * * *

What do you call kinky sex with chocolate?

S&M&M

10 WAYS TO KNOW YOU'VE HAD WILD SEX

1. Your mattress has turned into a giant sponge.
2. It takes five minutes to unknot your bodies.
3. An earthquake of 3.4 on the Richter Scale is recorded in your area.
4. The cat's exhausted from just watching you.
5. A trampoline company has to come to adjust your bed springs.
6. You've both gone down one clothing size.
7. You cancel your chiropractic appointment. There's nothing left to adjust.
8. You have to breathe into a brown paper bag.
9. Boy, are you hungry!
10. You're absolutely satisfied yet uncontrollably horny at the same time.

* * * * *

One day, this man, Tony, died. When he was sent to be judged, he was told that he had committed a sin, and that he could not go to heaven right away. He asked what he did and God told him that he cheated on his income taxes and that the only way he could get into heaven would be to sleep with a 500 pound, stupid, butt-ugly woman for the next five years and enjoy it. Tony decided that this was a small price to pay for an eternity in heaven. So off he went with this enormous woman, pretending to be happy.

As he was walking along, he saw his friend Carlos up ahead. Carlos was with an even bigger, uglier woman than he was with. When he approached Carlos he asked him what was going on, and Carlos replied, "I cheated on my income taxes and scammed the government out of a lot of money...even more then you did." They both shook their heads in understanding and figured that as long as they have to be with these women, they might as well hang out together to help pass the time.

Now Tony, Carlos, and their two beastly women were walking along, minding their own business when Tony and Carlos could have sworn that they saw their friend Jon up ahead, only this man was with an absolutely drop dead gorgeous supermodel/centrefold. Stunned, Tony and Carlos approached the man and in fact it was their friend Jon. They asked him how is he with this unbelievable goddess, while they were stuck with these god-awful women.

Jon replied, "I have no idea, and I'm definitely not complaining. This has been absolutely the best time of my life (and I'm dead,) and I have five years of the best sex any man could hope for to look forward to. There is only one thing that I can't seem to understand. After everytime we have sex, she rolls over and murmur's to herself, "Damn income taxes!"

* * * * *

One day this fellow noticed that a new couple had moved into the house next door. He was also quick to notice that the woman liked to sunbathe in the back yard, usually in a skimpy bikini that showed off a magnificent pair of breasts.

He made it a point to water and trim his lawn as much as possible, hoping for yet another look. Finally, he could stand it no more. Walking to the front door of the new neighbour's house, he knocked and waited. The husband, a large, burly man, opened the door. "Excuse me", our man stammered, "but I couldn't help noticing how beautiful your wife is."

"Yeah? So?" his hulking neighbour replied.

"Well, in particular, I am really struck by how beautiful her breasts are. I would gladly pay you ten thousand dollars if I could kiss those breasts." The burly gorilla is about to deck our poor guy when his wife appears and stops him. She pulls him inside and they discuss the offer for a few moments.

Finally, they return and ask our friend to step inside. "OK," the husband says gruffly, "for ten thousand dollars you can kiss my wife's breasts."

At this the wife unbuttons her blouse, and the twin objects of desire hang free at last. Our man takes one in each hand, and proceeds to rub his face against them in total ecstasy. This goes on for several minutes, until the husband gets annoyed. "Well, come on already, kiss 'em!" he growls.

"I can't." replies our awe-struck hero, still nuzzling away.

"Why not?" demands the husband, getting really angry now.

"I don't have ten thousand dollars!"

* * * * *

Q. How do you turn a fox into an elephant?
A. Marry it.

Q. How do you make five pounds of fat look good?
A. Give it a nipple.

Q. What do you call two lesbians in a canoe?
A. Fur traders.

There is this guy and this girl and they want to have sex. So they go to the girl's house and before entering the girl stops the guy and says.

"My little sister sleeps on the bottom bunk of our bunk bed and I do not want her to know what we are doing, so when I say 'baloney' it means push harder, and when I say 'pastrami' it means push slower."

With this the two get onto the top bunk and have sex. First, the girl moans, "baloney, baloney, baloney," then shouts "pastrami, pastrami, pastrami," and then back to "baloney,baloney,baloney."

Finally, the girls sister says "Will you guys quit making sandwiches up there, you're getting mayonnaise all over me!"

* * * * *

What's the last thing to go through a bug's mind as it hits the windsheild? His ass!

Q. What do Disney World and Viagra have in common?
A. They both make you wait an hour for a two minute ride.

Q. What's the definition of trust?
A. Two cannibals giving each other a blow job.

Q. Why is it called a Wonder Bra?
A. When she takes it off, you wonder where her tits went.

Q. Why does it take one million sperm to fertilise one egg?
A. They don't stop for directions.

Q. Did you hear about the flasher who was thinking of retiring?
A. He decided to stick it out for one more year!

Q. Barking dog at the back door wanting in and your wife's yelling at the front wanting in. Which one do you let in?
A. The dog, once he's in, he shuts up!

A businessman meets a beautiful girl and agrees to spend the afternoon with her for $500. So they do. Before he leaves, he tells her that he does not have any cash with him, but that he will have his secretary write a check and mail it to her, calling the payment, "RENT FOR APARTMENT."

On the way to the office he regrets what he has done, realising that the whole event was not worth the price. So he has his secretary send a check for $250 and enclosed the following typed note:

Dear Madam,

Enclosed find check in the amount of $250 for rent of your apartment. I am not sending the amount agreed upon, because when I rented the apartment, I was under the impression that:

1) it had never been occupied;
2) that there was plenty of heat;
3) that is was small enough to make me cozy and at home.

However, I found out that it had been previously occupied, that there wasn't any heat, and that it was entirely too large.

Upon receipt of the note, the girl immediately returned the check for $250 with the following note:

Dear Sir:

First of all, I cannot understand how you expect a beautiful apartment to remain unoccupied indefinitely. As for the heat, there is plenty of it, if you know how to turn it on. Regarding the space, the apartment is indeed of regular size, but if you don't have enough furniture to fill it, please do not blame the landlady.

* * * * *

Hear about the psychic midget who escaped from jail? Yeah the headlines in the newspaper read "SMALL MEDIUM AT LARGE".

* * * * *

Q. What do you call a virgin on a waterbed?
A. A cherry float.

Q. What does bungee jumping and hookers have in common?
A. They both cost a hundred bucks and if the rubber breaks, you're screwed.

During a Papal audience, a business man approached the Pope and made this offer: Change the last line of the Lord's prayer from, "give us this day our daily bread" to "give us this day our daily chicken." and KFC will donate 10 million dollars to Catholic charities. The Pope declined. Two weeks later the man approached the Pope again. This time with a 50 million dollar offer. Again the Pope declined. A month later the man offers 100 million, this time the Pope accepts. At a meeting of the Cardinals, The Pope announces his decision in the good news/bad news format. The good news is... that we have 100 million dollars for charities. The bad news is that we lost the Wonder Bread account!

* * * * *

Q. What's better than a rose on your piano?
A. Tulips on your organ.

Q. What did Adam say to Eve?
A. Stand back, I don't know how big this thing gets!

Q. How do you get a nun pregnant?
A. Dress her up as an alter boy.

A Jewish man walks into a bar and sits down. He has a few drinks, then he sees a chinese man and punches him in the face. "Owch!" the chinese man says. "What was that for?"

"That was for Pearl Harbor," the Jewish man says.

"But I'm Chinese!"

"Chinese, Japanese, what's the difference?" And the jewish man sits back down. Then, the chinese man walks up to the Jewish man and punches him in the face.

"Ouch!" the Jewish man says. "What was that for?"

"That was for the Titanic," the chinese man says.

"But that was an iceberg!"

"Ice berg, Goldberg, what's the difference?"

* * * * *

Q. What does parsley and pubic hair have in common?
A. Push it aside and keep on eating.

Q. How do you say 69 in Chinese?
A. Twocanchew (two can chew).

There was this businessman who was getting ready to go on a long business trip. He knew his wife was a flirtatious sort, so he thought he'd try to get her something to keep her occupied while he was gone, because he didn't much like the idea of her screwing someone else.

(For joke purposes, let's ignore what he might do while on his trip) So he went to a store that sold sex toys and started looking around. He thought about a life-sized sex doll but that was too close to another man for him. He was browsing through the dildos, looking for something special to please his wife, and started talking to the old man behind the counter. He explained his situation. The old man said, "Well, I don't really know of anything that will do the trick. We have vibrating dildos, special attachments, and so on, but I don't know of anything that will keep her occupied for weeks, except—and he stopped.

"Except what?" the man asked.

"Nothing, nothing."

"C'mon, tell me! I need something!"

"Well, sir, I don't usually mention this, but there is the voodoo dick."

"So what's up with this voodoo dick?" he asked. The old man reached under the counter, and pulled out an old wooden box, carved with strange symbols. He opened it, and there lay a very ordinary—looking dildo. The businessman laughed, and said "Big fucking deal. It looks like every other dildo in this shop!"

The old man replied, "But you haven't seen what it'll do yet." He pointed to a door and said, "Voodoo dick, the door." The voodoo dick rose out of its box, darted over to the door, and started screwing the keyhole. The whole door shook with the vibrations, and a crack developed down the middle. Before the door could split, the old man said, "Voodoo dick, get back in your box!" The voodoo dick stopped, floated back to the box and lay there, quiescent once more.

"I'll take it!" said the businessman. The old man resisted, saying it wasn't for sale, but he finally surrendered to $700 in cash. The guy took it home to his wife, told her it was a special dildo and that to use it, all she had to do was say "Voodoo dick, my pussy." He left for his trip satisfied that things would be fine while he was gone. After he'd been gone a few days, the wife was unbearably horny. She thought of several people who would willingly satisfy her, but then she remembered the voodoo dick. She got it out, and said "Voodoo dick, my pussy!" The voodoo dick shot to her crotch and started pumping. It was great, like nothing she'd ever experienced before. After three orgasms, she decided she'd had enough, and tried to pull it out, but it was stuck in her, still thrusting. She tried and tried to get it out, but nothing worked. Her husband had forgot to tell her how to shut it off. So she decided to go to the hospital to see if they could help. She put her clothes on, got in the car and started to drive to the hospital, quivering with every thrust of the dildo. On the way, another orgasm nearly made her swerve off the road, and she was pulled over by a policeman. He asked for her license, and then asked how much she'd had to drink. Gasping and twitching, she explained that she hadn't been drinking, but that a voodoo dick was stuck in her pussy, and wouldn't stop screwing. The officer looked at her for a second, and then said, "Yea, right. Voodoo dick, my ass!"

Facts about Women:

Women especially love a bargain. The question of 'need' is irrelevant, so don't bother pointing it out. Anything on sale is fair game.

Women never have anything to wear. Don't question the racks of clothes in the closet; you 'just don't understand'.

Women need to cry. And they won't do it alone unless they know you can hear them.

Women will always ask questions that have no right answer, in an effort to trap you into feeling guilty.

Women need to feel like there are people worse off than they are. That's why soap operas and Oprah Winfrey-type shows are so successful.

Women hate bugs. Even the strong-willed ones need a man around when there's a spider or a wasp involved.

Women can't keep secrets. They eat away at them from the inside. And they don't view it as being untrustworthy, providing they only tell two or three people.

Women always go to public restrooms in groups. It gives them a chance to gossip.

Women can't refuse to answer a ringing phone, no matter what she's doing. It might be the lottery calling!

Women never understand why men love toys. Men understand that they wouldn't need toys if women had an 'on/off' switch.

Women think all beer is the same.

Women keep three different shampoos and two different conditioners in the shower. After a woman showers, the bathroom will smell like a tropical rain forest.

Women don't understand the appeal of sports. Men seek entertainment that allows them to escape reality. Women seek entertainment that reminds them of how horrible things could be.

If a man goes on a seven-day trip, he'll pack five days worth of clothes and will wear some things twice; if a woman goes on a seven-day trip she'll pack 21 outfits because she doesn't know what she'll feel like wearing each day.

Women are paid less than men, except for one field: Modelling.

Women are never wrong. Apologising is the man's responsibility, 'It's there in the Bible.' Hmmm, who was it that gave Adam the apple?

Women do not know anything about cars. 'Oil-stick, oil doesn't stick?'

Women have better restrooms. They get the nice chairs and red carpet. Men just get a large bowl to share.

Women usually love cats. Men say they love cats, but when women aren't looking, men kick cats.

Women love to talk on the phone. A woman can visit her girlfriend for two weeks, and upon returning home, she will call the same friend and they will talk for three hours!

Women will drive miles out of their way to avoid the possibility of getting lost using a shortcut.

Women do NOT want an honest answer to the question, 'How do I look?'

PMS stands for: Permissible Man-Slaughter. (Or at least men think it means that. PMS also stands for Preposterous Mood Swings and Punish My Spouse.

The first naked man a woman sees is 'Ken'.

Women are insecure about their weight, butt and breast sizes.

Women will make left-hand turns to avoid making one right-hand turn.

'Oh, nothing,' has an entirely different meaning in woman-language than it does in man-language.

Lewis Carroll's Caterpillar had nothing on women.

Women cannot use a map without turning the map to correspond to the direction that they are heading.

All women are overweight by definition; don't agree with them about it. Women always have 5 kilos to lose, but don't bring this up unless they really have 5 kilos to gain.

If it is not Valentines day and you see a man in a flower shop, you can probably start up a conversation by asking, 'What did you do?'

Only women understand the reason for 'guest towels' and the 'good china'.

Women want equal rights, but you rarely hear them clamouring to be let into the draft to cover the responsibilities that go with those rights. All women seek equality with men until it comes to sharing the closet, taking out the trash, and picking up the check.

If a man ticks off a woman she will often respond by getting a fuzzy toilet cover which warms their rear, but makes it impossible for the lid to stay up thus it constantly gets peed on by the guys.

Women never check to see if the lid is up. They seem to prefer taking a flying butt leap towards the bowl and then chewing men out because they 'left the seat up' instead of taking two seconds and lowering it themselves.

Women don't really care about a sense of humour in a guy despite claims to the contrary. You don't see women trampling over Tom Cruise to get to Gilbert Gottfried, do you?

It's okay for women to dance with each other and not be gay. You don't see straight men dancing together.

Women will spend hours dressing up to go out, and then they'll go out and spend more time checking out other women. Men can never catch women checking out other men; women will always catch men checking out other women.

The most embarrassing thing for women is to find another woman wearing the same dress at a formal party. You don't hear men say, 'Oh NO!!!, there's another man wearing a black tux, get me out of here!'

Rules for Men...

1. The Female always makes The Rules.
2. The Rules are subject to change at any time without prior notification.
3. No Male can possibly know all The Rules.
4. If the Female suspects the Male knows all The Rules, she must immediately change some or all of The Rules.
5. The Female is NEVER wrong!
6. If the Female is wrong, it is because of a flagrant misunderstanding which was a direct result of something the Male did or said wrong.
7. If Rule 6 applies, the Male must apologise immediately for causing the misunderstanding.
8. The Female can change her mind at any given point in time.
9. The Male must never change his mind without express written consent from the Female.

10. The Female has every right to be angry or upset at any time.
11. The Male must remain calm at all times, unless the Female wants him to be angry or upset.
12. The Female must under no circumstances let the Male know whether or not she wants him to be angry or upset.
13. The Male is expected to mind read at all times.
14. The Male who doesn't abide by The Rules, can't take the heat, lacks a backbone, and is a wimp.
15. Any attempt to document The Rules could result in bodily harm.
16. At no time can the Male make such comments as "Insignificant" and "Is that all?" or "Finished?!" when the Female is complaining.
17. If the Female has PMS, all The Rules are null and void!

Great bumper stickers

* If You Can Read This, I've Lost My Trailer.
* The Earth Is Full—Go Home
* I Have The Body Of A God... Buddha
* This Would Be Really Funny If It Weren't Happening To Me
* Cleverly Disguised As A Responsible Adult
* If We Quit Voting Will They All Go Away?
* The Face Is Familiar But I Can't Quite Remember My Name
* Eat Right, Exercise, Die Anyway
* Honk If Anything Falls Off
* Cover Me, I'm Changing Lanes
* He Who Hesitates Is Not Only Lost But Miles From The Next Exit
* I Refuse To Have A Battle Of Wits With An Unarmed Person
* You! Out Of The Gene Pool!

* I Do Whatever My Rice Krispies Tell Me To
* It's Been Lovely But I Have To Scream Now
* I Haven't Lost My Mind, It's Backed Up On Disk Somewhere
* If You Can Read This, Please Flip Me Back Over..[Seen Upside Down, On A Jeep]
* Remember Folks: Stop Lights Timed For 35mph Are Also Timed For 70mph.
* If Walking Is So Good For You, Then Why Does My Mailman Look Like Jabba The Hut?
* Body By Nautilus; Brain By Mattel
* Boldly Going Nowhere
* Honk If You've Never Seen An Uzi Fired From A Car Window
* Money Isn't Everything, But It Sure Keeps The Kids In Touch
* You're Just Jealous Because The Voices Are Talking To Me

* Constipated People Don't Give A Shit.
* Practice Safe Sex, Go Screw Yourself.
* If You Drink Don't Park, Accidents Cause People.
* Who Lit The Fuse On Your Tampon?
* If You Don't Believe In Oral Sex, Keep Your Mouth Shut.
* Please Tell Your Pants Its Not Polite To Point.
* If That Phone Was Up Your Butt, Maybe You Could Drive A Little Better.
* My Kid Got Your Honor Roll Student Pregnant.
* To All You Virgins: Thanks For Nothing.
* If At First You Don't Succeed... Blame Someone Else And Seek Counselling.
* Impotence: Nature's Way Of Saying "No Hard Feelings".
* Horn Broken ... Watch For Finger.
* It's Not How You Pick Your Nose, But Where You Put The Booger.

* If You're Not A Haemorrhoid, Get Off My Ass.
* So Many Pedestrians—So Little Time
* Where Are We Going And Why Am I In This Handbasket?
* If Sex Is A Pain In The Ass, Then You're Doing It Wrong
* Fight Crime: Shoot Back!
* Guys: No Shirt, No Service—Gals: No Shirt, No Charge
* Necrophilia: That Uncontrollable Urge To Crack Open A Cold One.
* Ask Me About Ebonics
* Cat: The Other White Meat
* Caution - Driver Legally Blonde
* Don't Be Sexist - Bitches Hate That
* Heart Attacks ... God's Revenge For Eating His Animal Friends.
* How Many Roads Must A Man Travel Down Before He Admits He is lost?

* If You Can't Dazzle Them With Brilliance, Riddle Them With Bullets.
* Saw It ...Wanted It ...Had A Fit ...Got It!
* My Hockey Mom Can Beat Up Your Soccer Mom.
* GROW YOUR OWN DOPE—PLANT A MAN.
* All Men Are Animals, Some Just Make Better Pets.
* Some people are only alive because it is illegal to shoot them
* I used to have a handle on life, but it broke.
* WANTED: Meaningful overnight relationship.
* BEER: It's not just for breakfast anymore.
* So you're a feminist...Isn't that precious.
* I need somconc really bad...Are you really bad?
* Beauty is in the eye of the beer holder.

* * * * *

Q. What's the difference between a 'Spice Girls' video and a porn video?
A. The porn video has better music!

Q. What's the best part of having a homeless girlfriend?
A. You can drop her off where ever you want!

Q. Did you hear that the new and politically correct name for "lesbian".
A. It has been changed to "vagitarian".

Q. What's the definition of "Tender Love?"
A. Two gays with haemorrhoids.

Q. Did you hear about the two poofters who went to London?
A. They were REALLY pissed off when they found out Big Ben was a clock.

There is a sign in the drugstore window: "Condoms, custom fit."

So a man walks up to the counter and asks for a condom, like the sign says. The man at the counter tells him to see Edith in aisle 4. So the man finds Edith. Edith grabs the man by the crotch, then gets on the PA system and says, "Medium condom. Medium condom."

Well the man is embarrassed, but goes to the counter to get his condom.

Later, a second man sees the sign in the window, and goes up to the counter to get his condom. The druggist tells him to see Edith in aisle 4. Same thing happens, Edith grabs his crotch, gets on the PA and says, "Large condom, this man needs a large condom."

The man is pleased, at least, to be a large.

Next a teenager goes into the drugstore to get a fitted condom, and is told to see Edith is aisle 4. Edith grabs his crotch, gets on the PA and says, "Clean-up in aisle 4, clean-up in aisle 4."

How to Shower Like a Woman

1. Take off fourteen layers of clothing you put on this morning.
2. Walk to bathroom wearing robe and towel on head. If you happen to see boyfriend/husband along the way, ignore juvenile "turban-head" jokes and run to bathroom.
3. Look at womanly physique in the mirror and stick out stomach so as to complain about how fat you're getting.
4. Turn on hot water only.
5. Get in the shower—once you've found it through all the steam.
6. Look for facecloth, armcloth, legcloth, long loofah, wide loofah, and pumice stone.
7. Wash hair once with Cucumber and Lemon shampoo with 83 added vitamins.
8. Rinse hair.

9. Condition your hair with Cucumber and Lemon conditioner enhanced with natural crocus oil. Leave on hair for fifteen minutes.
10. Wash face with crushed apricot facial scrub for ten minutes until red and raw.
11. Try to wash entire rest of body with Ginger Nut and Java Cake bodywash.
12. Complain bitterly when you realise that your boyfriend/husband has once again been EATING your Ginger Nut and Java Cake body wash.
13. Rinse conditioner off hair (this takes at least fifteen minutes as you must make sure that all the conditioner has come off).
14. Debate shaving armpits and legs and decide that you can't be bothered.
15. Scream loudly when your boyfriend/husband flushes the toilet and you get a rush of cold water.
16. Turn hot water on full and rinse off.
17. Dry with a towel the size of a small African country.

How to Shower Like a Man

1. Take off clothes while sitting on the edge of the bed and leave them in a pile on the floor.
2. Walk to bathroom wearing a towel. If you see your girlfriend/wife along the way, flash her.
3. Look at your manly physique in the mirror and suck in your gut to see if you have pecs. No.
4. Turn on the water.
5. Check for pecs again. Still No.
6. Get in the shower.
7. Don't bother to look for a washcloth. You don't use one.
8. Wash your face.
9. Wash your armpits.
10. Wash your penis and surrounding area.
11. Wash your ass.
12. Shampoo your hair, do not use conditioner.

13. Make a shampoo mohawk.

14. Open the door and look at yourself in the mirror.

15. Pee.

16. Rinse off and get out of the shower.

17. Return to the bedroom wearing a towel, if you pass your girlfriend/wife, flash her.

* * * * *

Men's Mastercard Commercial

Cover Charge $15.00
Round of Drinks $23.00
Table Dance—$30.00
Another round of drinks $23.00
Couch dance and tips $50.00
A round of shots $34.00
Private dance in your hotel room $300.00
Being able to send her on her way and never have to hear her complain: PRICELESS.

Why it's Great To Be A Women

1. Free drinks.
2. Free dinners.
3. Free movies (you get the point).
4. You can hug your friend without wondering if she thinks you're gay.
5. You can hug your friend without wondering if YOU'RE gay.
6. You know The Truth about whether size matters.
7. Speeding ticket? What's that?
8. New lipstick gives you a whole new lease on life.
9. You never had to walk down the hall with your binder strategically positioned in high school.
10. If you have sex with someone and don't call them the next day, you're not the devil.
11. Condoms make no significant difference in your enjoyment of sex.
12. If you have to be home in time for Melrose Place, you can say so, out loud.
13. If you're not making enough money you can blame the glass ceiling.
14. You can sleep your way to the top.

15. You can sue the President for sexual harassment.
16. Nothing crucial can be cut off with one clean sweep.
17. It's possible to live your whole life without ever taking a group shower.
18. No fashion faux pas you make could rival The Speedo.
19. Brad Pitt.
20. You don't have to fart to amuse yourself.
21. If you cheat on your spouse, people assume it's because you're being emotionally neglected.
22. YOU never have to wonder if your orgasm was real.
23. You'll never have to decide where to hide your nose-hair clipper.
24. No one passes out when you take off your shoes.
25. If you think the person you're dating really likes you, you don't have to break up with them.
26. Excitement is only as far away as the nearest beauty-supply store.
27. If you forget to shave, no one has to know.
28. You can congratulate your teammate without ever touching her butt.
29. If you have a zit, you can conceal it.

30. You never have to reach down every so often to make sure your privates are still there.
31. If you're dumb, some people will find it cute.
32. You don't have to memorise Caddyshack or Fletch to fit in.
33. You have the ability to dress yourself.
34. You have an excuse to be a total bitch at least once a month.
35. You can talk to people of the opposite sex without having to picture them naked.
36. If you marry someone 20 years younger, you're aware that you look like an idiot.
37. If you're wearing cologne, you don't have to pretend it's aftershave.
38. You'll probably never see someone you know while peeing in an alley.
39. You'll never have to punch a hole through anything with your fist.
40. You can quickly end any fight by crying.
41. Your friends won't think you're weird if you ask whether there's spinach in your teeth.

42. There are times when chocolate really can solve all your problems.
43. You've never had a goatee.
44. Gay waiters don't make you uncomfortable.
45. You'll never regret piercing your ears.
46. You can fully assess a person just by looking at their shoes.
47. You'll never discover you've been duped by a Wonderbra.
48. You don't have hair on your back.
49. You know which glass was yours by the lipstick mark.
51. You get to hate Kathie Lee in the way only another woman truly can.

* * * * *

Q. Why are roach clips called roach clips?
A. Because "pot holder" was already taken.

Q. What's the worst part about getting a lung transplant?
A. The first couple of times you cough, its not your phlegm.

Things Men Should Know

1. The reason our bras don't always match our underwear is because WE actually CHANGE our underwear.
2. The next time you and your buddies joke about armed women in combat, take a poll to see which of you successfully aim at the toilet bowl.
3. If we're watching football with you, it's not bonding. We're watching because of the butts.
4. If the truth hurts, ask us those ego-sensitive questions on your payday.
5. Whenever possible, please try to say whatever you have to say after the movie.
6. Don't fret if you find out that the postman delivers more than once a day.
7. Please don't drive when you're not driving.
8. Lay off the beans several hours before bedtime.
9. Our bedtime headaches are inversely proportional to the number of baths that you take.
10. If you were really looking for an honest answer you wouldn't ask in bed.

11. The next time you joke about female drivers, research the number of accidents caused by rubbernecking at miniskirts.
12. If only women gossip, how do you and your buddies keep track of "who's easy?"
13. Stop telling us that most male strippers are gay: WE DON'T CARE!
14. Start parting and combing your hair to one side early in life: You'll never see the island coming.
15. Have a strong need for male bonding? Visit your proctologist.
16. Your contributions to your child should go above and beyond that chromosome you unselfishly sacrificed.
17. Eye contact is best established above our shoulder level.

* * * * *

Nicknames:-

If Gloria, Suzanne, Debra and Michelle go out for lunch, they will call each other Gloria, Suzanne, Debra and Michelle. But if Mike, Phil, Rob and Jack go out for a brewsky, they will affectionately refer to each other as Bullet-Head, Godzilla, Peanut-Head and Useless.

Eating Out:-

And when the check comes, Mike, Phil, Rob and Jack will each throw in $20 bills, even though it's only for $22.50. None of them will have anything smaller, and none will actually admit they want change back. When the girls get their check, out come the pocket calculators.

Bathrooms:-

A man has six items in his bathroom—a toothbrush, shaving cream, razor, a bar of Dial soap, and a towel from the Holiday Inn.The average number of items in the typical woman's bathroom is 437. A man would not be able to identify most of these items.

Groceries:-

A woman makes a list of things she needs and then goes out to the store and buys these things. When finished, she goes to the shortest checkout line. A man waits till the only items left in his fridge are half a lime and a beer. Then he goes grocery shopping. He buys everything that looks good. By the time a man reaches the checkout counter, his cart is packed tighter than the Clampett's car on Beverly Hillbillies. Of course, this will not stop him from going to the 10-items-or-less lane. But usually, he will go to the lane with the cutest check-out girl regardless of how long the line is.

Shoes:-

When preparing for work, a woman will put on a Mondi wool suit, then slip on Reebok sneakers. She will carry her dress shoes in a plastic bag from Saks. When a woman gets to work, she will put on her dress shoes. Five minutes later, she will kick them off because her feet are under the desk. A man will wear the same pair of shoes all day.

Offspring:-

Ah, children. A woman knows all about her children. She knows about dentist appointments and soccer games and romances and best friends and favourite foods and secret fears and hopes and dreams. A man is vaguely aware of some short people living in the house that often ask him for money or the keys to the car.

Laundry:-

Women do laundry every couple of days. A man will wear every article of clothing he owns, including his surgical pants that were hip about eight years ago, before he will do his laundry. When he is finally out of clothes, he will wear a dirty sweatshirt inside out, rent a U-Haul and take his mountain of clothes to the Laundromat. Men always expect to meet beautiful women at the Laundromat.

Dressing:-

A woman will dress up to: go shopping, water the plants, empty the garbage, answer the phone, read a book, get the mail. A man will dress up for: weddings, funerals.

The Technique

Leaving the poker party late, as usual, two friends compared notes. "I can never fool my wife," the first complained. "I turn off the car's engine and coast into the garage, take off my shoes, sneak upstairs, and undress in the bathroom. But she always wakes up and yells at me for being out so late and leaving her alone."

"You got the wrong technique my friend," his buddy replied. "I roar into the garage, slam the door, stomp up the steps, rub my hand on her ass and say 'How about a little?' She always pretends to be asleep."

* * * * *

Q. Why did God invent yeast infection?
A. So women know what it feels like to live with an annoying c**t.

Q. Did you hear about the two gay guys that had an argument in the bar?
A. They went outside to exchange blows.

Because We Are Men

If you put a woman on a pedestal and try to protect her from the Rat Race, you're a Male Chauvinist Pig.

If you stay home and do the housework, you're a pansy.

If you work too hard, there is never any time for her and the kids.

If you don't work enough, you're a good-for-nothing layabout.

If she has a boring repetitive job with low pay, this is exploitation.

If you have a boring repetitive job with low pay, you should get off your ass and find something better.

If you get a promotion ahead of her, that is favouritism.

If she gets a job ahead of you, it's equal opportunity.

If you mention how nice she looks, it's sexual harassment.

If you keep quiet, it's male indifference.

If you cry, you're a sheila.

If you don't, you're an insensitive bastard.

If you thump her, it's wife-bashing.

If she thumps you, it's self-defense.

If you make a decision without consulting her, you're a chauvinist.

If she makes a decision without consulting you, she's a liberated woman.

If you ask her to do something she doesn't enjoy, that's domination.

If she asks you, it's a favour.

If you appreciate the female form and frilly underwear, you're a pervert.

If you don't, you're a poofter.

If you like a woman to shave her legs and keep in shape, you're sexist.

If you don't, you're unromantic.

If you try to keep yourself in shape, you're vain.

If you don't, you're a slob.

If you buy her flowers, you're after something.

If you don't, you're not thoughtful.

If you're proud of your achievements, you're up yourself.

If you don't, you're not ambitious.

If you ask for a cuddle, you never think of anything but sex.

If you're totally whacked after a hard day's work, you don't give a stuff about other people's needs.

If she has a headache, she's tired.

If you have a headache, you don't love her any more.

If you want it too often, you're oversexed.

If you don't, there must be someone else.

* * * * *

Dad and The Maid

Little Johnny came home early from school and started calling his mother with no answer. He finally went up stairs and saw the bedroom door was open a little. When he peered in, he saw his dad on the bed with the maid so he quietly went outside and waited for his mother. When she showed up with some groceries, he said "Mommy, Mommy guess what I saw? I saw daddy upstairs on the bed with the maid and they were..." and his Mother said, "Stop right there, Johnny." Wait until supper tonight when the maid is serving the meal. When I wink at you, then tell me the story."

At supper when all were seated and being served by the maid, she winked and Johnny began again. "Mommy, when I got home from school early today, I was looking for you and saw daddy on the bed with the maid. They were doing the same thing that I saw you and Uncle Phil doing at the cottage last summer."

Reliving Old Times

A husband and wife are out for a drive through the countryside. They reach a familiar spot and the wife says, "Sweetheart, let's do the same thing we did here forty years ago!" The husband stops the car. His wife backs against the fence, and he immediately jumps her like a bass on a June bug. They make love like never before. She was SCREAMING and GYRATING and SHAKING uncontrollably; and when it was over, much to her husband's surprise, she FAINTED! After he revived her and got her back into the car, the husband, quite astounded says: "Darlin', you sure never moved like that forty years ago—or ANYTIME SINCE that I can remember." The woman, gasping for breath, finally able to speak, says: "FORTY YEARS AGO THAT DARN FENCE WASN'T ELECTRIFIED!"

Their First Night Together

On their first night to be together, the newlywed couple go to get changed. The new bride comes out of the bathroom, all showered and wearing her beautiful robe. The proud husband says, "My dear, we are married now, you can open your robe."

The beautiful young woman opens her robe, and he is astonished. "Oh, oh, aaaahhh," he exclaims, "My word, you are so beautiful, let me take your picture. Puzzled, she asks, "My picture?"

He answers, "Yes my dear, so I can carry your beauty next to my heart forever."

She smiles and he takes her picture, and then he heads into the bathroom to shower.

He comes out wearing his robe and the new wife asks, "Why do you wear a robe? We are married now."

At that the man opens his robe and she exclaims, "Oh, oh, oh my, let me get a picture."

He beams and asks, "Why?"

She answers, "So I can get it enlarged."

The Lazy Husband

A husband is at home watching a football game when his wife interrupts, "Honey, could you fix the light in the hallway? It's been flickering for weeks now."

He looks at her and says angrily, "Fix the light? Now? Does it look like I have a G.E. logo printed on my forehead? I don't think so."

"Well then, could you fix the fridge door? It won't close right."

To which he replied, "Fix the fridge door? Does it look like I have Westinghouse written on my forehead? I don't think so."

"Fine," she says, "Then could you at least fix the steps to the front door? They're about to break."

"I'm not a damn carpenter and I don't want to fix the steps," he says. "Does it look like I have Ace Hardware written on my forehead? I don't think so. I've had enough of you. I'm going to the bar!"

So he goes to the bar and drinks for a couple hours. He starts to feel guilty about how he treated his wife, and decides to go home and help out. As he walks into the house, he notices the steps are already fixed. As he enters the house, he sees the hall light is working. As he goes to get a beer, he notices the fridge door is fixed. "Honey, how'd this all get fixed?"

She said, "Well, when you left, I sat outside and cried. Just then a nice young man asked me what was wrong, and I told him. He offered to do all the repairs, and all I had to do was either screw him or bake him a cake." He said, "So, what kind of cake did you bake him?"

She replied, "Hellooooo... Do you see Betty Crocker written on my forehead?"

* * * * *

Q. Why is a woman's pussy like a warm toilet seat?
A. They both feel good, but you wonder who was there before you.

Q. What is the first sign of AIDS?
A. A pounding sensation in the ass.

Q. What did Cinderella do when she got to the ball?
A. Gagged.

Old Things

A wife arrived home after a long shopping trip, and was horrified to find her husband in bed with a young, lovely thing. Just as she was about to storm out of the house, her husband stopped her with these words: "Before you leave, I want you to hear how this all came about. Driving home, I saw this young girl, looking poor and tired, I offered her a ride. She was hungry, so I brought her home and fed her some of the roast you had forgotten about in the refrigerator. Her shoes were worn out so I gave her a pair of your shoes you didn't wear because they were out of style. She was cold so I gave her that new birthday sweater you never wore even once because the colour didn't suit you. Her slacks were worn out so I gave her a pair of yours that you don't fit into anymore. Then as she was about to leave the house, she paused and asked, 'Is there anything else that your wife doesn't use anymore?' "And so, here we are!"

The Five Kinds of Sex

The first is Smurf Sex. This happens during the honeymoon; you both keep doing it until you're blue in the face.

The second is Kitchen Sex. This is at the beginning of the marriage; you'll have sex anywhere, anytime. Including the kitchen.

The third kind is Bedroom Sex. You've calmed down a bit, perhaps have kids, so you've got to do it in the bedroom.

The fourth kind is Hallway Sex. This is where you pass each other in the hallway and say, "Fuck you!"

There is also a fifth kind of sex: Courtroom Sex. This is when you get divorced and your wife fucks you in front of everyone in the court.

* * * * *

Benefits of Alzheimer's

An 85 year old man marries a lovely 25 year old woman. Because her new husband is so old the woman decides that on their wedding night they should have separate suites. She is concerned that the old fellow could overexert himself. After the festivities she prepares herself for bed and for the knock on the door she is expecting. Sure enough the knock comes and there is her groom ready for action. They unite in conjugal union and all goes well whereupon he takes his leave of her and she prepares to go to sleep for the night. After a few minutes there's a knock on the door and there the old guy is again ready for more action. Somewhat surprised she consents to further coupling which is again successful after which the octogenarian bids her a fond good night and leaves. She is certainly ready for slumber at this point and is close to sleep for the second time when there is another knock at the door and there he is again fresh as a 25 year old and ready for more. Once again they do the horizontal boogie. As they're lying in afterglow the young bride says to him, "I am really impressed that a guy your age has enough juice to go for it three times. I've been with guys less than half your age who were only good for one." The old guy looks puzzled and turns to her and says, "Was I already here?

* * * * *

The Chicken or The Egg

A chicken and an egg are lying in bed. The chicken is smoking a cigarette with a satisfied smile on its face and the egg is frowning and looking put out. The egg mutters upset to no one in particular "I guess we answered THAT question."

* * * * *

Q. What's the last thing Tickle Me Elmo receives before he leaves the factory?
A. Two test tickles.

Q. What is the definition of a menstrual period?
A. A bloody waste of fucking time.

Old Age Divorce

A 54 year old accountant leaves a letter for his wife one Friday evening that reads:

Dear Wife (that's what he called her):
I am 54 and by the time you receive this letter I will be at the Grand Hotel with my beautiful and sexy 18 year old secretary. When he arrived at the hotel there was a letter waiting for him that read as follows:

Dear Husband (that's what she called him):
I too am 54 and by the time you receive this letter I will be at the Breakwater Hotel with my handsome and virile 18 year old toy boy. You being an accountant will therefore appreciate that 18 goes into 54 many more times than 54 goes into 18.

* * * * *

Q. What do women and police cars have in common?
A. They both make a lot of noise to let you know they are coming.

Ask Your Mother

A mother and her son were flying "Southwest Airlines" from Kansas to Chicago. The son (who had been looking out the window) turned to his mother and said, "If big dogs have baby dogs and big cats have baby cats, why don't big planes have baby planes?"
The father (who couldn't think of an answer) told her son to ask his mother.
So the boy asked his mother , "If big dogs have baby dogs and big cats have baby cats, why don't big planes have baby planes?"
His Mother asked, "Did your father tell you to ask me?" He said that she had. So she said, "Tell your father that Southwest always pulls out on time."

* * * * *

Q. What is the difference between pussy and apple pie?
A. You can eat your mom's apple pie.

Q. Why do women pierce their bellybutton?
A. Place to hang their air freshener.

Ask Before Marriage

A man met a beautiful lady and he decided he wanted to marry her right away. She said, "But we don't know anything about each other."
He said, "That's all right, we'll learn about each other as we go along." So she consented, and they were married, and went on a honeymoon to a very nice resort. So one morning they were lying by the pool, when he got up off of his towel, climbed up to the 10 metre board and did a two and a half tuck gainer, this followed by a three rotations in jackknife position, where he straightened out and cut the water like a knife. After a few more demonstrations, he came back and laid down on the towel. She said, "That was incredible!"
He said, "I used to be an Olympic diving champion. You see, I told you we'd learn more about ourselves as we went along." So she got up, jumped in the pool, and started doing laps. After about thirty laps she climbed back out and laid down on her towel hardly out of breath.
He said, "That was incredible! Were you an Olympic endurance swimmer?"
"No," she said, "I was a hooker in Venice and I worked both sides of the canal.

Don't Argue With The Wife

A man and his wife were having a heated argument at breakfast. As he stormed out of the house, the man angrily yelled to his wife, "You aren't that good in bed either!" By midmorning, he decided he'd better make amends and phoned home. After many rings, his wife, clearly out of breath, answered the phone.

"What took you so long to answer and why are you panting?"

"I was in bed."

"What in the world are you doing in bed at this hour?"

"Getting a second opinion."

* * * * *

Q. How do you teach a blond math?
A. Subtract her clothes, divide her legs, and square root her.

Q. What did the paedophile say when he got out of jail?
A. I feel like a kid again!

Why Chocolate is Better than Sex

1) You can GET chocolate.
2) "If you love me you'll swallow that" has real meaning with chocolate.
3) Chocolate satisfies even when it has gone soft.
4) You can safely have chocolate while you are driving.
5) You can make chocolate last as long as you want it to.
6) You can have chocolate even in front of your mother.
7) If you bite the nuts too hard the chocolate won't mind.
8) Two people of the same sex can have chocolate without being called nasty names.
9) The word "commitment" doesn't scare off chocolate.
10) You can have chocolate on top of your workbench/desk during working hours without upsetting your co-workers.
11) You can ask a stranger for chocolate without getting your face slapped.

12) You don't get hairs in your mouth with chocolate.

13) With chocolate there's no need to fake it.

14) Chocolate doesn't make you pregnant.

15) You can have chocolate at any time of the month.

16) Good chocolate is easy to find.

17) You can have as many kinds of chocolate as you can handle.

18) You are never too young or too old for chocolate.

19) When you have chocolate it does not keep your neighbours awake.

20) With chocolate size doesn't matter.

* * * * *

The Modern Boyfriend

A 65 year old woman came home one day and heard strange noises in her bedroom. She opened the door and discovered her 40 year old daughter playing with a vibrator. "What on earth are you doing?" asked the Mom.

"Mom, I am 40 years old and look at me. I am ugly. I will never get married, so this is pretty much my husband." The mother walked out of the room, shaking her head in disgust. A couple of days later, the father comes home from work. He also hears a strange noise coming from the bedroom. Upon entering the room found his daughter using the vibrator. "What the hell are you doing?" he asked.

His daughter replied, "I already told Mom. I am 40 years old now and ugly. I will never get married so this is as close as I'll ever get to a husband."

The father walked out of the room shaking his head too. One Sunday, the Mother came home to find her husband watching the Super Bowl. He had a beer in one hand, and the vibrator in the other hand "Bloody Hell, what are you doing?" she cried.

The husband replied "What does it look like I'm doing? I'm having a beer and watching the game with my son-in-law!"

* * * * *

Mother-In-Law

There was a married couple who were in a terrible accident. The woman's face was burned severely. The doctor told the husband they couldn't graft any skin from her body because she was so skinny. The husband then donated some of his skin...however, the only place suitable to the doctor was from his buttocks. The husband requested that no one be told of this, because after all this was a very delicate matter! After the surgery was completed, everyone was astounded at the woman's new beauty. She looked more beautiful than she ever did before! All her friends and relatives just ranted and raved at her youthful beauty. She was alone with her husband one day and she wanted to thank him for what he did.

She said, "Dear, I just want to thank you for everything you did for me! There is no way I could ever repay you!"

He replied, "Oh don't worry, Honey, I get plenty thanks every time your mother comes over and kisses you on your cheek!"

* * * * *

Condoms

A father and his son go into the grocery store when they happen upon the condom aisle. The son asks his father why there are so many different boxes of condoms. The father replies, Well, you see that 3 pack? That's for when you're in high school. You have 2 for Friday night and 1 for Saturday night. The son then asks his father, well what's the 6 pack for? The father replies, well that's for when you're in college. You have 2 for Friday night, 2 for Saturday night, and 2 for Sunday morning. Then the son asks his father what the 12 pack is for. The father replies, well that's for when you're married. You have one for January, one for February, one for March...

I admire your strength, I admire your spunk
But the thing I like best, is getting you drunk.

Our love will never become cold and hollow
Unless, one day, you refuse to swallow.

This feels so good, it feels so right
I just wish it wasn't $250 a night.

You're a woman of style, you're a woman of class
Especially when I'm spanking, your big-round-fat ass.

Before I met you, my heart was so famished
But now I'm fulfilled... SO MAKE ME A SAMICH!

Through all the things that came to pass
Our love has grown...but so's your ass.

You're a honey and you're a cutie
I just wished you had J-Lo's "booty".

I don't wanna be sappy or silly or corny
So, right to the point, let's do it, I'm horny!

If you think that hickey looks like a blister,
you should check out the one that I gave to your sister!

Things to do when bored in a megamart

1. Get boxes of condoms and randomly put them in people's carts when they don't realise it.
2. Set all the alarm clocks to go off at ten minute intervals throughout the day.
3. Make a trail of orange juice on the floor, leading to the rest rooms.
4. Walk up to an employee and tell him in an official tone, "I think we've got a Code 3 in house wares," and see what happens.
5. Tune all the radios to a polka station; then turn them all off and turn the volumes to full.
6. Challenge other customers to duels with tubes of gift wrap.
7. Put M&M's on lay-by.
8. Move "Caution: Wet Floor" signs to carpeted areas.
9. Set up a tent in the camping department; tell others you'll only invite them in if they bring pillows from Bed and Bath.
10. When someone asks if you need help, begin to cry and ask, 'Why won't you people just leave me alone?'

11. Look right into the security camera, and use it as a mirror while you pick your nose.
12. Take up an entire aisle in Toys by setting up a full scale battlefield with G.I. Joes vs. the X-Men.
13. Ask other customers if they have any Dijon Mustard.
14. While handling guns in the hunting department, suddenly ask the clerk if he knows where the anti-depressants are.
15. Switch the men's and women's signs on the doors of the rest rooms.
16. Dart around suspiciously while humming the theme from "Mission Impossible."
17. Set up a "Valet Parking" sign in front of the store.
18. In the auto department, practice your "Madonna" look with various funnels.
19. Hide in the clothing racks and when people browse through, say things like "Pick me! Pick me!!"
20. When an announcement comes over the loudspeaker, assume the fetal position and scream, "No, no! It's those voices again!"
21. Go into the dressing room and yell real loud, "Hey, we're out of toilet paper in here!"

Wisdom From Kids

"Never trust a dog to watch your food."—Patrick, age 10

"Never tell your Mom her diet's not working."—Michael, age 14

"Stay away from prunes." —Randy, age 9

"Don't pull Dad's finger when he tells you to."—Emily, age 10

"When your Mom is mad at your Dad, don't let her brush your hair."—Taylia, age 11

"Never let your three-year old brother in the same room as your school assignment."—Traci, age 14

"A puppy always has bad breath—even after eating a Tic-Tac."—Andrew, age 9

"Never hold a dustbuster and a cat at the same time." —Kyoyo, age 11

"You can't hide a piece of broccoli in a glass of milk." —Amir, age 9

"Don't wear polka-dot underwear under white shorts." —Kellie, age 11

"If you want a kitten, start out by asking for a horse."—Naomi, age 15

"Felt-tip markers are not good to use as lipstick." —Lauren, age 9

"Don't pick on your sister when she's holding a baseball bat."—Joel, age 10

"When you get a bad grade in school, show it to your Mom when she's on the phone."—Alyesha, age 13

"Never try to baptise a cat."—Eileen, age 8

* * * * *

Q. Why did the gay guy think his lover was cheating on him?

A. He came home shit faced.

Q. What do you get when you cross a rooster with a flea?

A. An itchy cock.

Q. Why is a Laundromat a bad place for a guy to pick up women?

A. Women who can't even afford a washing machine will never be able to support you.

The following are a sampling of REAL answers received on exams given by the California Department of Transportation's traffic school.

Q: Do you yield when a blind pedestrian is crossing the road?
A: What for? He can't see my license plate.

Q: Who has the right of way when four cars approach a four-way stop at the same time?
A: The pick up truck with the gun rack and the bumper sticker saying, "Guns don't kill people. I do."

Q: What are the important safety tips to remember when backing your car?
A: Always wear a condom.

Q: When driving through fog, what should you use?
A: Your car.

Q: How can you reduce the possibility of having an accident?
A: Be too shit-faced to find your keys.

Q: What problems would you face if you were arrested for drunk driving?
A: I'd probably lose my buzz a lot faster.

Q: What changes would occur in your lifestyle if you could no longer drive lawfully?
A: I would be forced to drive unlawfully.

Q: What is the difference between a flashing red traffic light and a flashing yellow traffic light?
A: The colour.

Q: How do you deal with heavy traffic?
A: Heavy psychedelics.

Q: What can you do to help ease a heavy traffic problem?
A: Carry loaded weapons.

Q: Why would it be difficult to be a police officer?
A: It would be tough to be a dickhead all day long.

* * * * *

Top Tips From Viz

If a small child is choking on an ice cube, don't panic. Simply pour a jug of boiling water down its throat and hey presto! The blockage is almost instantly removed.

Clumsy? Avoid cutting yourself while slicing vegetables by getting someone else to hold them while you chop away.

Keep the seat next to you on the train vacant by smiling and nodding at people as they walk up the aisle.

Weight watchers. Avoid that devilish temptation to nibble at the chocolate bar in the cupboard or fridge by not buying the f**king thing in the first place, you fat bastards.

Save on booze by drinking cold tea instead of whisky. The following morning you can create the effects of a hangover by drinking a thimble full of washing up liquid and banging your head repeatedly on the wall.

Make bath times as much fun for kiddies as a visit to the seaside by pouring a bucket of sand, a bag of salt and a dog turd into the bath.

Recreate the fun of a visit to a public swimming pool in your own home by filling the bath with cold water, adding two bottles of bleach, then urinating into it, before jumping in.

Girls: Too old to go on an 18 to 30 holiday? Simply get pissed, lie in a sand pit in your garden and shag every bloke who looks at you ovcr the fence.

Don't buy expensive 'ribbed' condoms, just buy an ordinary one and slip a handful of frozen peas inside it before you put it on.

X-Files fans: Create the effect of being abducted by aliens by drinking two bottles of vodka. You'll invariably wake up in a strange place the following morning, having had your memory mysteriously 'erased'.

Don't waste money buying expensive binoculars. Simply stand closer to the object you wish to view.

Putting just the right amount of gin in your goldfish bowl makes the fishes' eyes bulge and cause them to swim in an amusing manner.

Save time when crossing a one-way street by only looking in the direction of oncoming traffic.

Thicken up runny low-fat yoghurt by stirring in a spoonful of lard.

Anorexics: When your knees become fatter than your legs, start eating cakes again.

A next door neighbour's car aerial, carefully folded, makes an ideal coat hanger in an emergency.

An empty aluminium cigar tube filled with angry wasps makes an inexpensive vibrator.

Olympic athletes: Disguise the fact that you've taken anabolic steroids by running a bit slower.

Avoid an asymmetrical bulge in your right arm by masturbating furiously with your left arm too.

Avoid arguments with the missus about lifting the loo seat by simply pissing in the sink.

Weedy fellas: Develop a right forearm like Arnold Schwarzenegger by buying one of those Cindy Crawford workout videos.

Smokers: Save on matches and lighters, by simply lighting your next fag from the butt of your last one.

Vegetarians coming to dinner? Simply serve them a nice bit of steak or veal. Since they're always going on about how tofu, Quorn, meat substitute etc tastes exactly like the real thing, they won't know any difference.

Invited by vegetarians for dinner? Point out that since you'd no doubt be made aware of their special dietary requirements, tell them about yours, and ask for a nice steak.

Before attempting to remove stubborn stains from a garment always circle the stain in permanent pen so that when you remove the garment from the washing machine you can easily locate the area of the stain and check that it has gone.

Give comics that 'Pulp Fiction' feel by reading the last frames of cartoons first, then reading the rest in a random order.

High blood pressure sufferers: Simply cut yourself and bleed for a while, thus reducing the pressure in your veins.

Heavy smokers: Don't throw away those filters from the end of your cigarettes. Save them up and within a few years you'll have enough to insulate your loft.

Motorists. Enjoy the freedom of cycling by removing your windscreen, sticking half a melon skin on you head, then jumping red lights and driving the wrong way up one way streets.

Create instant designer stubble by sucking a magnet and dipping your chin in a bowl of iron fillings.

Convince neighbours that you have invented a 'SHRINKING' device by ruffling your hair, wearing a white laboratory coat and parking a Haulpak or similar outside your house for a few days. Then dim and flicker the lights in your house during the night and replace the Haulpak unseen, with a Tonka toy of the same description. Watch their faces in the morning!

Have all your shits at work. Not only will you save money on toilet paper, but you'll also be getting paid for it.

Small car drivers: Attach a lighted sparkler to the roof of your car before starting a long journey. You drive the things like dodgem cars anyway, so it may as well look like one.

A mouse trap, placed on top on of your alarm clock will prevent you from rolling over and going back to sleep.

* * * * *

A guy and a girl are having sex when they both say, "I'm really hungry and thirsty too." It was freakin' freezing in the house so they both have an argument over who should go get the food and drink.

After a while they decide to have a contest. Whoever can come up with the best poem would be the one to stay in bed.

They both think for a while when the guy says, "Okay, I got one. Two times two is four plus five is nine, I can pee in yours but you can't pee in mine".

So she thinks for a minute and says, "Okay two times two is four plus five is nine, I know the length of yours but you'll never know the depth of mine."

Top Ten Reasons Men Won't Say "I Love You"

1. They don't mean it.
2. They want to get laid, but not 'that' bad.
3. Their fathers didn't say it to their mothers.
4. It has become a throw-away phrase.
5. They don't want to be trapped in some long-term thing.
6. They've said it before and found out they were wrong.
7. They think it is much cooler to say it to other men, like Sammy and Frank.
8. It will lead to "I'll marry you".
9. There is an outside chance they will be rejected.
10. If they say it, their genitals will fall off.

Top Ten Reasons Women Want Men To Say "I Love You"

1. They like the words.
2. Girls, at times, think that the "words" are important.
3. They can brag to their friends that they got him to do it.
4. It makes them feel all tingly to hear it.
5. Commitment/Power
6. He ain't gettin' ANY unless he does.
7. It makes up for what a jerk he is the rest of the time.
8. It makes sex better.
9. The woman can say it back without risking rejection.
10. The woman wants to see his genitals fall off.

Two Deaf People

Two deaf people get married. During the first week of marriage, they find that they are unable to communicate in the bedroom when they turn off the lights (because they can't see each other using sign language). After several nights of fumbling around and misunderstandings, the wife proposes a solution."Honey," she signs,"Why don't we agree on some simple signals? For instance, at night, if you want to have sex with me, reach over and squeeze my left breast one time. If you don't want to have sex, reach over and squeeze my right breast one time." The husband thinks this is a great idea and signs back to his wife, "Great idea! Now if you want to have sex with ME, reach over and pull on my penis one time. And if you don't want to have sex, reach over and pull on my penis...fifty times."

Relationship Building by Examples

Husband and wife are getting all snugly in bed. The passion is heating up. But then the wife stops and says "I don't feel like it, I just want you to hold me."

The husband says "WHAT?"

The wife explains that he must not be in tune with her emotional needs as a Woman. The husband realises that nothing is going to happen tonight and he might as well deal with it. So the next day the husband takes her shopping at a big department store. He walks around and has her try on three very expensive outfits. And then tells his wife. We'll take all three of them. Then goes over and gets matching shoes worth $200 each. And then goes to the Jewellery department. and gets a set of diamond earrings. The wife is so excited (she thinks her husband has flipped out, but she does not care). She goes for the tennis bracelet. The husband says, "but you don't even play tennis, but OK if you like it then lets get it." The wife is jumping up and down so excited she cannot even believe what is going on. She says, "I am ready to go, lets go to the cash register."

The husband says, "no—no—no, honey we're not going to buy all this stuff." The wife's face goes blank. "No honey—I just want you to HOLD this stuff for a while." Her face gets really red and she is about to explode and then the Husband says, "You must not be in tune with my financial needs as a Man!"

* * * * *

Q. What's gray, sits at the bed and takes the piss?
A. A kidney dialysis machine.

Q. What do you call a female police officer that shaves her pubic hair?
A. C**t Stubble.

Q. Why do only 10% of women go to heaven?
A. Because if they all went, it would be hell.

Q. What goes: "CLICK -is that it? CLICK -is that it? CLICK -is that it?"
A. A blind person with a rubix cube.

From The Mouths of Babes

A teacher was working with a group of children, trying to broaden their horizons through sensory exploration. With their eyes closed, they would feel objects from stones to pine cones and smell aromatic herbs and exotic fruits. Then one day, the teacher brought in a great variety of lifesavers, more flavours than you could imagine. "Children, I'd like you to close your eyes and taste these," announced the teacher. Without difficulty, they managed to identify the taste of cherries, lemons, and mint but when the teacher had then put honey flavoured lifesavers in their mouths, every one of the children were stumped. "I'll give you a hint," said the teacher. "It's something your Daddy and Mommy probably call each other all the time." Instantly, one of the children spat the lifesaver out of his mouth and shouted, "Spit 'em out you guys, they're assholes!"

* * * * *

Letter to My Wife/Husband

To My Dear Wife,

During the past year, I have tried to make love to you 365 times. I have succeeded 12 times. The following list is why I didn't often succeed.

1. The sheets are clean—54 times
2. It is too late—17 times
3. Too tired from shopping all day—49 times
4. It is too early—20 times
5. It is too hot—15 times
6. Pretending to be asleep—15 times
7. The neighbours will hear us—3 times
8. Headache—22 times
9. Sunburn—7 times
10. Your Mother will hear us—9 times
11. Not in the mood—43 times
12. You will wake the baby—17 times
13. Watching the late show—6 times
14. New Hairdo—5 times
15. Too sore—16 times
16. Wrong time of month—36 times
17. Have to get up early—19 times

Of the 12 times I did succeed, the activity was not satisfactory because 2 times you just laid there, 4 times you reminded me that there was a crack in the ceiling, 3 times you told me to hurry up and get it over with, 2 times I had to wake you up to tell you that I had finished, and once I was afraid I had hurt you because I felt you move.

To My Dear Husband,

I think that you have gotten things a little confused. Here are the real reasons you did not get it more often than you did.

1. Came home drunk and tried to fuck the cat—15 times
2. Did not come home at all—36 times
3. Did not come—21 times
4. Came too soon—33 times
5. Went soft before you got it in—33 times
6. Toes cramped—10 times
7. Working too late—38 times
8. Have to get up early to play golf—29 times
9. Had a fight and someone kicked you in the balls —2 times

10. Caught Herman in your zipper—4 times
11. Caught a cold and your nose kept running—3 times
12. Burned your tongue on hot coffee—3 times
13. You had a splinter in your finger—2 times
14. Came in your PJ's while reading a dirty book—16 times
15. Watching football on TV—98 times
16. Haemorrhoids flared up—10 times

Of the times we did get together, the reason I laid still was because you were fucking the sheets. I wasn't talking about the crack in the ceiling. What I said was, would you prefer me on my back or kneeling. The time you felt me move was because you farted and I was trying to breathe!

* * * * *

Q. Did you hear Cher is joining the spice girls?
A. They're going to call her Old Spice.

Q. What do you do when your dishwasher stops working?
A. Yell at her.

Q. What's the difference between oral sex and anal sex?
A. Oral sex makes your day, anal sex makes your hole weak.

Q. Why do female skydivers wear jock straps?
A. So they don't whistle on the way down.

Q. Why did the woman cross the road?
A. Never mind that, what the fuck is she doing out of the kitchen?

Q. Why do women have 2% more brains than a cow?
A. So, when you pull their tits they won't shit on the floor.

Q. Why can't women read maps?
A. Because only the male mind can comprehend the concept of 1 inch equals a mile.

Q. What is better than a cold Bud?
A. A warm bush.

The Perfect Day According To: HER

8:45 Wake up to hugs and kisses.
9:00 5 pounds lighter on the scale.
9:30 Light breakfast.
11:00 Sunbathe.
12:30 Lunch with best friend at outdoor cafe.
1:45 Shopping.
2:30 Run into boyfriend's/husband's ex—notice she's gained 30 lbs.
3:00 Facial, massage, nap.
7:30 Candlelight dinner for two and dancing.
10:00 Make love.
11:30 Pillow talk in his big strong arms.

* * * * *

The Perfect Day According To: HIM

10:00 Wake up.
10:02 Oral sex.
10:10 Big breakfast.
11:30 Drive up coast in Ferrari with gorgeous babe with big hooters.
2:15 Enormous lunch.
3:15 Oral sex.
3:25 Play sports with the guys.
4:30 Drink beer with the guys.
6:30 Meet Claudia Schiffer.
6:40 Oral sex.
6:50 Huge dinner, more beer.
11:00 Full on, get down, gorilla sex.
11:10 Sleep.

* * * * *

Q. What do you get when you cross a rooster and peanut butter?
A. A cock that sticks to the roof of your mouth.

Q. Why did God create alcohol?
A. So ugly people would have a chance to have sex.

Q. Why do women prefer old gynaecologists?
A. Their shaky hands!

Q. What do you do if your girlfriend starts smoking?
A. Slow down and use some lubricant.

Q. Why are women like Kentucky Fried Chicken?
A. After you've finished with the thigh and breasts, all you have left is a greasy box to put your bone in.

Q. What does a bull do to stay warm on a bitterly cold day?
A. He goes into the barn and slips into a nice warm "Jersey"

Q. What do you call an open can of tuna in a lesbian's apartment?
A. Potpourri

Q. What does tightrope walking and getting a blowjob from Grandma have in common ?
A. You don't look down.

Q. Who can make more money in a week, a drug dealer or a prostitute?
A. The prostitute because she can wash and resell her crack.

Q. How are a lawyer and a prostitute different?
A. The prostitute stops fucking you after you're dead.

Q. What has one hundred balls and screws old ladies?
A. Bingo

Q. What is a zebra?
A. 26 sizes larger than an "A" bra.

Q. What did the blind man say as he passed the fish market?
A. Good morning Girls

Q. What's the difference between a woman and a fridge?
A. A fridge doesn't fart when you pull your meat out!

Q. How is being at a singles bar different than being at the circus?
A. At the circus, the clowns don't talk.

Q. How many newspapers can a woman hold between her legs?
A. One Post, two Globes, and many Times.

Q. Did ya hear about the new "morning after" pill for men?
A. It works by changing your blood type!!

Q. What do you call a truck full of dildos?
A. Toys for Twats

Q. How do you get four old ladies to shout "Fuck"?
A. Get a fifth old lady to shout "Bingo!"

Q. What is the difference between a female snowman and a male snowman?
A. Snowballs.

Q. How many men does it take to open a beer bottle?
A. None. It should be open when she brings it to you.

Q. What do you call it when a 90 year old man masturbates successfully?
A. Miracle whip.

Q. What's the definition of macho?
A. Jogging home from your own vasectomy.

Q. What do women and milk cartons have in common?
A. You gotta open the flaps to get to the good stuff.

Q. Why do bunnies have soft sex?
A. They have cotton balls.

Q. What happens when you kiss a canary?
A. You get chirpes, it can't be tweeted because its a canarial disease.

Q. What does the receptionist at the sperm clinic say to clients as they are leaving?
A. Thanks for coming.

Q. How do you know when you honeymoon is over?
A. When he no longer smiles as he scrapes the burnt toast.

Q. What do a gynaecologist and a pizza delivery boy have in common?
A. They can both smell it, but can't eat it.

Q. You know why they say that eating oysters will improve a man's sex life?
A. Because women know if he'll eat one of those, he'll eat anything!

Q. What is the definition of "making love"?
A. Something a woman does while a guy is fucking her.

Q. What's the only animal with an asshole in the middle of its back?
A. A police horse.

Q. What does it mean when the flag at the Post Office is flying at half mast?
A. They're hiring.

Q. Did you hear Richard Simmons had plastic surgery to get his love handles removed?
A. Yeah...now he has no ears.

Q. Do you know how to eat a frog?
A. You put one leg over each ear.

Q. How are fat girls and mopeds alike?
A. They are fun to ride but you don't want your friends to find out.

Q. How do you fuck a fat chick?
A. Roll her in flour and find the wet spot.

Q. Why is it difficult to find men who are sensitive, caring, and good looking?
A. They already have boyfriends.

Q. Why is sleeping with a man like a soap opera?
A. Just when it's getting interesting, they're finished until next time.

Q. What do you call a guy who never farts in public?
A. A private tutor.

Q. What do you call a musician without a girlfriend?
A. Homeless.

Q. What has 2 gray legs and 2 brown legs?
A. An elephant with diarrhoea.

Q. Why did the Avon lady walk funny?
A. Her lipstick.

Q. What does the cannibal do just after he dumped his girlfriend?
A. Wiped his ass.

Q. What is the smallest hotel in the world?
A. A pussy, cause you have to leave the bags outside.

Q. What do a toilet and a woman have in common?
A. Without the hole in the middle they aren't good for shit.

Q. How can you tell a tough lesbian bar?
A. Even the pool table has no balls.

Q. What do you call a lesbian with fat fingers?
A. Well hung.

Q. What two words will clear out a men's changing room quicker than anything else?
A. Nice dick!

Q. How do you know when a Barbie has her period?
A. All your tic tacs are gone.

Q. What happened to the Pope when he went to Mount Olive?
A. Popeye almost killed him!

Q. How can you tell a head nurse?
A. She's the one with the dirty knees!

Q. What do you call three lesbians in bed together?
A. Ménage é twat.

Q. What do you call hemorrhoids on a fag?
A. Speed bumps.

Q. What is the lightest thing in the world?
A. A penis...even a thought can raise it.

Q. What do gay kids get for Christmas?
A. Erection Sets.

Q. Where do fags park?
A. In the rear.

Q. What is the difference between a man buying a lottery ticket and a man fighting with his wife?
A. A man has a chance at winning at the lottery.

Q. What does a female snail say during sex?
A. Faster, faster, faster!

Q. What is the noisiest thing in the world?
A. Two skeletons screwing on a tin roof.

Q. What's red and blue with a long string?
A. A smurfette with her period.

Q. What do you call an adolescent rabbit?
A. A pubic hair.

Q. Define "Egghead."
A. What Mrs. Dumpty gives to Humpty.

Q. How can you tell if you have acne?
A. If the blind can read your face.

Q. Did you know they just discovered a new use for sheep in New Zealand?
A. Wool!

Q. What's a necrophiliac's biggest complaint about sex?
A. They just kinda lay there.

Q. What did the woman say to her swimming instructor?
A."Will I really drown if you take your finger out?"

Q. Why did the lumber truck stop?
A. To let the lumber jack off.

Q. Why did the woman get thrown out of the riding stable?
A. She wanted to mount the horse her way.

Q. Hey, what's sticky, white and falls from the sky?
A. The cumming of the Lord

Q. How did the tugboat get AIDS?
A. It was rear-ended by a ferry.

Q. How can you tell a sumo wrestler from a feminist?
A. A Sumo wrestler shaves his legs.

Q. What's the difference between a bandleader and a gynaecologist?
A. A bandleader fucks his singers and a gynaecologist sucks his fingers.

Q. Do you know what the square root of 69 is?
A. Ate something.

Q. What is the difference between "Oooh!" and "Aaah!"?
A. About three inches.

Q. What do you do in case of fallout?
A. Put it back in and take shorter strokes!

Q. Why do women have two holes so close together?
A. In case you miss.

Q. When does a Cub Scout become a Boy Scout?
A. When he eats his first Brownie.

Q. How can you tell when an auto mechanic just had sex?
A. One of his fingers is clean.

Q. Why does a penis have a hole in the end?
A. So men can be open minded.

Q. What's the biggest fish in the world?
A. A horse, if you catch one you can eat her for months.

Q. How can you tell if your girlfriend wants you?
A. When you put your hand down her pants and it feels like you're feeding a horse.

Q. Have you heard about the new 'Mint' flavoured birth control pill for women that they take immediately before sex?
A. They're called 'Predickamints'

Q. What is the difference between a golf ball and a g-spot?
A. Men will spend two hours searching for a golf ball.

Q. What's the difference between a toad and a horny toad
A. One goes "ribbit" the other goes "rub it".

Q. Did you hear about the guy who finally figured out women?
A. He died laughing before he could tell anybody.

Q. What's the difference between Mad Cow disease and PMS?
A. Nothing.

Q. How do you confuse a female archaeologist?
A. Give her a used tampon and ask her what period it's from.

Q. Why does the bride always wear white?
A. Well aren't all kitchen appliances that colour?

Q. What's the difference between parsley and pussy?
A. Nobody eats parsley.

Q. What's green, slimy and smells like Miss Piggy?
A. Kermit's finger

Q. What do you do with 365 used rubbers?
A. Melt them down, make a tire, and call it a Goodyear.

Q. What's the difference between sin and shame?
A. It is a sin to put it in, but it's a shame to pull it out.

Q. What's the speed limit of sex?
A. 68 because at 69 you have to turn around.

Q. Why did Frosty the Snowman pull down his pants?
A. He heard the snow blower coming.

Q: What do you call a lesbian dinosaur?
A: Lickalotopuss.

Q. What do the spice girls and a pack of M&Ms have in common?
A. There are assorted colours, but they all taste the same.

Q. What do you call an Amish guy with his hand up a horses ass?
A. A mechanic.

Q. What do you call an Alabama farmer with a sheep under each arm?
A. Pimp.

Q. What do Eskimos get from sitting on the ice too long?
A. Polaroids.

Q. Why are women like tires?
A. There's always a spare.

Q. What's brown and sits on a piano bench?
A. Beethoven's First Movement.

Q. What do you call a nun with a sex change operation?
A. A tran-sister.

Q. What did one gay sperm say to the other gay sperm?
A. I can't see a thing with all this shit in here!

Q. Why do women wear black underwear?
A. They are mourning for the stiff they buried the night before.

Q. How do you know when a male porn star is at the gas station?
A. Right before the gas stops pumping he pulls out the nozzle and sprays it all over the car.

Q. What is the difference between a hockey game and a High School reunion?
A. At a hockey game you see fast pucks.

Q. What do you call a vegetarian with diarrhoea?
A. A salad shooter.

Q. Why did the boy fall off the swing?
A. He didn't have any arms.

Q. Why do women have arms?
A. Have you any idea how long it would take to LICK a bathroom clean?

Q. Why is being in the military like a blowjob?
A. The closer you get to discharge, the better you feel.

Q. What's the bad news about being a test tube baby?
A. You know for sure that your dad is a wanker.

Q. How are men like noodles?
A. They're always in hot water, they lack taste, and they need dough.

Q. Why don't Canadians have group sex?
A. Too many thank-you letters to write afterwards.

Q. Why are hangovers better than women?
A. Hangovers will go away.

Q. How many honest, intelligent, caring men in the world does it take to do the dishes?
A. Both of them.